★ SPORTS STARS ★

SAMMY SOSA
CUBS CLUBBER

BY CALEB MacLEAN

Children's Press®
A Division of Grolier Publishing
New York London Hong Kong Sydney
Danbury, Connecticut

Photo Credits

Photographs ©: AllSport USA: 20, 27 top, 44 right (Jonathan Daniel), 6 (Elsa Hasch), 37, 38 (Vincent Laforet); AP/Wide World Photos: 19, 23, 33, 44 left; Archive Photos: 31 (Reuters/Gary Caskey), 12 (Reuters/Zoraida Díaz), 42, 45 right (Reuters/Larry Downing), 40 (Reuters/HO), 11, 35 (Reuters/Onorio Montás), 41 (Reuters/Sue Ogrocki); Corbis-Bettmann: 43 (Agence France Presse); Sports Illustrated Picture Collection: 28 (Time Inc./John Biever); SportsChrome East/West: cover, 47 (Jeff Carlick), 25, 45 left, 46 (Rob Tringali Jr.); Tom DiPace: 3, 16, 27 bottom.

Visit Children's Press® on the Internet at:
http://publishing.grolier.com

Library of Congress Cataloging-in-Publication Data

MacLean, Caleb.
    Sammy Sosa : cubs clubber / by Caleb MacLean.
      p. cm. — (Sports stars)
    Summary: A biography of the Chicago Cubs power hitter, Sammy Sosa, from his poor childhood in the Dominican Republic to the home run record-breaking 1998 season.
    ISBN 0-516-21662-7 (lib.bdg.)   0-516-27005-2(pbk.)
    1. Sosa, Sammy, 1968-   Juvenile literature. 2. Baseball players— Dominican Republic Biography Juvenile literature. [1. Baseball players.] I. Title. II. Title: Sammy Sosa. III. Series.
GV865.S59M33 1999
796.357'092—dc21
[B]—dc21
                                    99-23005
                                       CIP
                                       AC

✷ CONTENTS ✷

☆ 1 ☆

TEAM PLAYER

The fans in the Wrigley Field bleachers are on their feet cheering, even though the inning has not yet started. They are greeting their right fielder, Sammy Sosa, who is running across the grass toward the ballpark's ivy-covered walls. As he gets closer, the volume increases, until he reaches his position. Sammy blows a kiss to his fans, gives them his familiar "V for Victory" sign, then pounds his heart to let them know he loves them back.

The first batter lines a pitch into the right-field alley. Sammy sprints to his right and considers diving for the ball. Not worth the gamble, he decides. Instead, he plays the ball off the wall and fires a bullet to the second baseman, who whirls around and throws out the runner sliding into third base. Sammy will not make any headlines with this play. But he knows it is just as important as one of his long home runs. Hitting homers and setting records is fun, but for Sammy, winning has always been number one.

★ 2 ★

JUST SCRAPING BY

On the island nation of the Dominican Republic, there is a city of roughly 125,000 people called San Pedro de Macorís. Through the years, it has produced a lot of major leaguers, including Rico Carty, Pedro Guerrero, George Bell, and Tony Fernandez. But if you think that it is some kind of baseball "paradise," you are wrong. San Pedro is one of the most impoverished cities in the Caribbean. Sometimes, the only thing that keeps the people from giving up is the enormous pride they have in the young men they have sent to the majors. These sports heroes' exploits fuel the dreams of thousands of Dominican kids, most of whom are too poor to own a proper glove, bat, or ball.

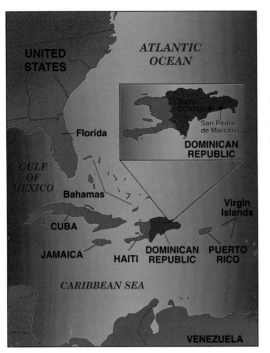

Sammy has come a long way from the poverty of his childhood, but he has never forgotten the people of the Dominican Republic.

Sammy Sosa was one of these boys back in the 1980s. His father, John, died unexpectedly of a brain aneurysm in 1976, eight years after Sammy was born. Sammy's mother had to raise him and his six siblings on her own. Mireya Sosa worked as a maid, and the other children did whatever they could to help the family survive. Sammy shined shoes, sold fruit, and did odd jobs to make a dollar or two a week. "It wasn't so long ago that Sammy Sosa was a nobody," he likes to say.

One day, Sammy and his younger brother, Jose, saw a woman take a bite from an apple and then throw it away. It was rotten. Sammy asked the woman if he could have it to bring it back to his mother. She was so touched that she asked her husband—a businessman named Bill Chase—to help Sammy out. Chase already knew Sammy well. Wherever he went, the boy seemed to appear out of thin air, asking him for a job. In time, Chase became Sammy's "second father." He gave some money to the family and bought

Sammy's mother, Mireya, still lives in the Dominican Republic, but she never misses a Cubs game.

Thanks to Sammy, the children of San Pedro can now learn baseball at the modern facility he constructed.

Sammy his first real baseball equipment. Before that, he used a mitt made out of a milk carton and played barefoot.

Soon Sammy showed enough potential to approach Hector Peguero, who ran a local youth league. Peguero gave private lessons to some of the more talented boys. Sammy said he could not afford Peguero's fee, but once Hector saw the boy's big shoulders, huge hands, and boundless enthusiasm, he decided he would teach him for free. After just a few months, everyone was talking about "El Gago"—the kid with the stutter who could hit the ball a mile and run like the wind.

Three teams—the Philadelphia Phillies, Toronto Blue Jays, and Texas Rangers—had scouts watching Sammy, who was now 15 years old. Each believed Sammy had enough raw, natural talent that he could be molded into a superstar. The first team to approach Sammy was the Phillies. In the fall of 1984, they tried to sign him prior to his 16th birthday, which was against the rules. Anxious to bring money into the Sosa home, he signed anyway. The contract was later cancelled. After Sammy turned 16, the Blue Jays and Rangers moved in. Each club had a facility in the Dominican Republic, and each team gave Sammy a tryout. At first it looked as if Sammy would sign with Toronto. But Mireya Sosa liked and trusted Texas scout Omar Minaya. When the Rangers offered a $3,500 bonus, Sammy signed on the dotted line. He bought himself a bicycle—the first he had ever owned—and gave the rest of the money to his mother.

NEW LAND, NEW WAYS

Sammy began his professional career in the spring of 1986, playing for the Gulf Coast Rangers of the Florida State League. He struck up a relationship with two other Spanish-speaking teenagers on the team, shortstop Rey Sanchez and outfielder Juan Gonzalez. Sammy's manager in 1986 was Rudy Jamarillo. He took the three players aside and explained to them that even though they were heroes back home, to baseball fans in the United States, they were nothing until they made the big leagues. This was not the time to relax, Jamarillo said, but the time to work twice as hard as they ever had in their lives. Because he had received no formal coaching until age 14, Sammy had to work harder than anyone on the basics of baseball. He cursed Jamarillo and called him the Devil behind his back. But years later Sammy credited his first manager with showing him what it took to become a superstar. "We were young guys, and we knew we could play this game," Sammy remembers. "After we got there, we realized we had to go out there every day, work on our hitting, and take fly balls every day."

Sammy's first season was an encouraging one. He led the league in doubles and total bases and threw out nine runners in 61 games. Over the next two seasons, he moved up one level each year and improved his power, speed, and defense. Sammy was beginning to feel comfortable in the field and on the bases, but at the plate, he always seemed to be a step behind the pitchers. He could not distinguish between fastballs and off-speed pitches, and he had trouble judging whether

Unlike many major-league sluggers, Sammy has not lost the blazing speed he possessed as a teenager.

pitches would be strikes or not. Sammy would simply wait as long as he could and then lash his bat at the ball. Sometimes he produced screaming line drives for doubles, triples, and homers. More often, however, he hit weak pop-ups and grounders or simply struck out.

At the start of the 1989 season, Sammy was promoted to the Tulsa Drillers of the Double-A Texas League, two levels below the majors. The Rangers watched his progress closely, for he had never faced pitching this good before. Sammy got off to a fast start, hitting right around .300 over the first ten weeks. In mid-June, the Rangers found themselves in a four-way battle for the American League Western Division lead. They needed a special player who could shake things up and move them in front of the pack. They told Sammy to pack his bags and join the team. It was the chance of a lifetime.

★ 4 ★

MAKING THE MAJORS

Sammy played his first major-league game on June 16, 1989, at New York's Yankee Stadium. He got a single and a double. Five days later, he hit a home run off Boston Red Sox ace Roger Clemens. Unfortunately, Sammy's success did not last long. Pitchers learned how to use his aggressiveness against him and began making him look foolish. The Rangers sent him back to the minors while they tried to put together a trade for the player they needed to win the division. That player turned out to be Harold Baines of the Chicago White Sox, an excellent clutch hitter. The Rangers decided to trade Sammy and pitcher Wilson Alvarez to get Baines.

Sammy gets a "low five" from Cecil Espy after his first major-league game, as fellow Dominican Julio Franco looks on.

The following spring, Sammy won Chicago's starting rightfield job and played well all year. He hit for power and stole a lot of bases. Sammy also was the only player in the league to reach double-figures in doubles, triples, and home runs.

Sammy relaxes in his new uniform. The 1989 trade to the White Sox gave him a chance to play every day.

He still chased after far too many bad pitches, though, and he refused to hit the ball to the opposite field. But the White Sox believed those skills would develop in time.

Chicago assumed that Sammy would be a key part of the pennant run they intended to make in 1991. They had two other rising stars in Frank Thomas and Robin Ventura, plus a good, young pitching staff. Sammy began the year with a bang, smashing a pair of homers against the Orioles on Opening Day. After that, however, it was all downhill. He was swinging harder and thinking less, and the result was a batting average in the low .200s. In July, he was shipped to the minors. When he returned to the White Sox later in the season, he mostly sat on the bench. Chicago could no longer afford to let Sammy learn on the job.

★ 5 ★

LEARNING THE GAME

Prior to the 1992 season, the White Sox got
an offer for Sammy they could not refuse.
George Bell, a veteran, dependable power hitter,
had worn out his welcome with the Chicago Cubs,
and the Cubs were looking for a dynamic young
player like Sammy. The Sosa-for-Bell trade was
made at the end of spring training. At first, it
looked as if the White Sox had gotten the better
of the deal. Bell hammered 25 homers and had
112 RBIs for the South Siders in 1992, while on
the North Side of Chicago, Sammy missed nearly
100 games with a fractured ankle and broken
wrist. Cubs fans were furious. Just like many

other times in their history, the Cubs had traded away a player who went on to have a great year, while the guy they got in return had landed on the junk pile. Sammy burned to show the fans they were wrong. But he could do nothing until the 1993 season started.

One of the true marks of an all-around baseball player is membership in the "30-30 club"—players who combine for at least 30 homers and 30 stolen

Sammy is all smiles on his first day with the Cubs. Batting coach Billy Williams (right) worked with Sammy to make him a complete hitter.

bases in the same season. Baseball fans had long recognized that Sammy possessed the potential to join this club, but it wasn't until 1993 that he learned the discipline to reach this level. Cubs' batting coach Billy Williams worked with Sammy to unleash his potential. Williams explained that the sooner you recognize what type of pitch is coming, the quicker you can decide what to do with it. Sammy learned that for every pitch, there was an "ideal" reaction, and for most pitches the ideal reaction is to let it go by— something he rarely did.

Slowly but surely, Sammy began to see the ball better and make smarter decisions. The result was the kind of year that everyone had been waiting for: 33 home runs, 36 stolen bases, and a .261 batting average. At last, Sammy Sosa was fulfilling the potential everyone had been talking about. As a 30-30 man, he had entered an elite class of baseball stars.

Sammy eyes the catcher as he breaks for third base. His 36 steals in 1993 earned him membership in the "30-30 club."

Sammy's numbers continued to improve in 1994 and 1995. In 1996, he already had amassed 40 home runs by mid-August, and people were abuzz over whether he might challenge Roger Maris's single-season home-run record of 61. But then a broken hand ended Sammy's season with six weeks to go.

Despite his shortened season, Cubs fans fell in love with Sammy. At the start of each inning, he would run to his position and acknowledge their cheers. The ever-devoted "Bleacher Bums," who watched Sammy every day from Wrigley Field's right-field bleachers, would bow when he took his position after hitting a home run. Sammy was always available after games and on off days for autographs or an appearance for a worthy cause. "Fans appreciate me because I work hard and try to contribute on defense when I'm not hitting," Sammy says. "I try to be a complete player in the outfield, at the plate, on the bases. If I have a problem, I find it and correct it."

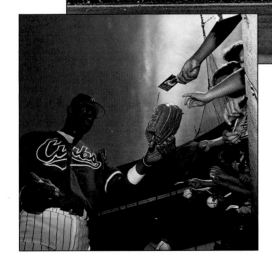

Sammy likes to connect with the Wrigley Field fans, both before and during games.

Sammy watches the ball rocket off his bat. His big swing also produces a lot of strikeouts.

Prior to the 1997 season, the Chicago Cubs decided to reward Sammy with a $42.5 million contract extension. It was the team's way of letting him know that they wanted him. It also was a sign to the fans that the Cubs were willing to spend money to put good players on the field. Sammy now had plenty of money to make sure his family would be taken care of forever. There was even enough to start a charitable foundation and fund construction projects back in San Pedro.

Instead of relaxing, however, Sammy began worrying that he was not worth all that money. He felt he had to be Superman instead of himself. Every time Sammy came to the plate, he tried to do too much. Once the pitchers saw this, he was dead. So for much of the 1997 season, Sammy looked like the raw rookie who had broken into the big leagues back in 1989. "I was trying to hit two home runs in every at bat," he remembers, still angry at his stupidity.

Sammy's statistics for 1997 do not look too bad at first glance. He hit more than 30 homers and knocked in more than 100 runs. But he led the league with 174 strikeouts and his on-base percentage was horrible. Some fans were furious. They thought Sammy had stopped trying. Manager Jim Riggleman and the other players were disappointed, too. They had hoped Sammy would step up and become a leader.

☆ 6 ☆

A FRESH START

Sammy came to spring training in 1998 ready to erase the bad memories of 1997. The team was looking good, and he was ready to be the player everyone expected the season before. Sammy had spent the winter watching films of himself and other top sluggers. He noticed that he swung much harder than they did. This gave him little chance of making solid contact with curveballs and sliders. Sammy worked on slowing down his swing and recognizing pitches sooner. A result of this new approach was that he stopped swinging at bad balls. "When I take those pitches," explains Sammy, "they say, 'This guy only goes for pitches over home plate. I have to throw him a strike.' "

Now seeing quality strikes for the first time in his career, Sammy felt great at the plate. In April, he slammed six balls out of the park; in May, he clubbed another seven. Then, suddenly, everything came together. Sammy went on a slugging

Sammy cools off during an August 1998 game. He ended the month tied with Mark McGwire in the home-run race.

rampage. He hit seven homers during the first eight days of June. Five days later, he hit three in one day. On June 25, Sammy hit his 19th homer of the month to tie the record established by Detroit Tiger catcher Rudy York in 1937. Five days later, in his last at bat of the month, Sammy hit his 20th home run of June to set a new record. That gave him 33 homers on the season, just four behind St. Louis Cardinals' first baseman Mark McGwire.

Until Sammy's historic hot streak, McGwire had been the primary focus of attention in baseball. He was making a run at Roger Maris's single-season record of 61 homers. Now the two players would chase the record together. For the rest of the summer, tens of millions of fans charted their progress. Some of these people had followed baseball for many years, while others were new to the game. Many had stopped watching baseball after a labor dispute ruined the 1994 season, vowing never to return. Sammy and Mark brought them back and captured the imagination of fans throughout the world as they matched each other blast-for-blast through July and August. They were doing more than challenging baseball's most famous record; they were making the game fun again.

Roger Maris connects for his 61st home run of the 1961 season, shattering Babe Ruth's 34-year-old record. Maris's mark held up for 37 years.

A SEPTEMBER
TO REMEMBER

On the morning of September 1, 1998, Sammy Sosa and Mark McGwire were tied with 55 home runs. The big debate was no longer whether Maris's record would fall, but which slugger would be the first to break it—and who would end up winning the home-run title. Most people picked McGwire. The Cardinals were out of the race in the N.L. Central, so he had little to concern him other than knocking the ball out of the park. The Cubs were in a tense struggle for a playoff position, so there were times when Sammy was called upon to sacrifice his power for the good of the team. This added up to a slight advantage for McGwire.

As the schedule wore on, something else happened that would reduce Sammy's chances of winning the home-run battle. Hurricane Georges rolled over the Caribbean and made a direct hit on the Dominican Republic. San Pedro de Macorís was nearly wiped off the map. When Sammy saw the first pictures of his hometown in the newspapers, he burst into tears. It looked as

San Pedro lays in ruins after Hurricane Georges passes over the Dominican Republic. Sammy wept when he first saw pictures like this one.

if a nuclear bomb had been dropped. Over the remaining weeks of the season, the fate of his friends and family in San Pedro was constantly on his mind. Between games, he tried to organize a relief effort for the island. Understandably, during games, his concentration was not always sharp. "Every minute, every at bat, I suffered thinking of my people," he admits.

Somehow, Sammy managed to keep pace with McGwire. The Cardinals' first baseman was the first to reach 61, and he hit 62 on September 8 to break the record. Ironically, McGwire's blast came in a game against the Cubs, and after the record-setting homer, Sammy trotted in from right field to congratulate his friend and fellow slugger.

But after watching McGwire make history, Sammy stormed right back, catching McGwire on September 23 with home run number 65. Two days later, Sammy hit a 410-foot shot off of Houston's Jose Lima to take the lead with 66. But later that day, McGwire tied him. Sammy hit

Sammy congratulates Mark McGwire after his 62nd homer. Sammy reached 62 against the Brewers five days later.

no more home runs in 1998, while McGwire had a big final weekend, hitting four against the Expos to finish with 70. It was a breathtaking conclusion to the most memorable season ever.

The "Bleacher Bums" go wild as Sammy sprints to his position during the one-game playoff against the Giants.

But the season was *not* over. The Cubs and
Giants finished the schedule with identical
records, forcing a single playoff game for the
N.L. Wild Card. In that contest at Wrigley Field,
San Francisco pitchers refused to give Sammy
anything he could drive, so he settled for a pair
of singles and scored two runs to lead the Cubs
to a 5-3 victory. It was a joyous night for long-
suffering Cubs fans, who had seen their team
reach the postseason only two times in more
than 50 years. But the joy ended quickly, for in
the first round of the playoffs, the Cubs faced
the Atlanta Braves, who had the best starting
pitchers in baseball. The Braves swept the Cubs
and put a quick finish to their glorious year.

Sammy's 1998 season will go down
as one of the great individual performances in
the history of baseball. Along with his 66 round-
trippers, he collected 158 RBIs, which is more
than anyone had gotten since 1949. Sammy also
led the majors with 132 runs scored. On paper,
his year was just a notch below McGwire's. But in

Mark and Sammy make the cover of *Sports Illustrated* as 1998 Sportsmen of the Year.

reality, Sammy's season was baseball's best. In December, he was named the National League's Most Valuable Player. It was a storybook ending, and he knew it. "I wish everyone could touch my heart and feel what I've felt," he says. "What happened to me . . . is the best thing that could ever happen to a human being."

Those close to Sammy say that the weeks following the season were more important to him than the season itself. He never stopped working to help his people. Sammy scheduled fund-raising stops in New York and Miami before returning home, and collected more than 250 tons of food, medicine, and clothing. He also raised $400,000 in cash. When he arrived in Santo Domingo,

Sosa gives fans his trademark "V for Victory" sign after being named the league's Most Valuable Player.

thousands of people followed him everywhere he went, lining the roads for miles whenever he traveled. Many of those cheering him were among the 100,000 left homeless by Hurricane Georges. Sammy Sosa is all they had left. Why did he get

First Lady Hillary Rodham Clinton applauds Sammy at President Clinton's 1998 State of Union address.

so personally involved after such a long and exhausting season? Why didn't he just send a check and make a few phone calls? "I am in debt to my pueblo of San Pedro de Macorís," he explains, "the land that saw me born and helped me grow."

When Sammy looks back on his great season and the months that followed, it is sometimes hard for him to believe what he accomplished. He will not say whether he thinks he can top his performance—or whether he even wants to try! What Sammy will say is what baseball fans have been saying themselves ever since: "Nineteen ninety-eight . . . what a year, what a year."

Sammy takes his hat off to the fans. Without their love and support, he says, he never would have made it through the 1998 season.

C ★ H ★ R ★ O ★ N

1968 • Sammy Sosa is born in San Pedro de Macorís, Dominican Republic.

1976 • Sammy's father dies.

1983 • Sammy begins playing organized baseball.

1985 • Sammy is signed by the Texas Rangers at the age of 16

1989 • Sammy makes his major-league debut for the Texas Rangers in June; he is traded to the Chicago White Sox in July.

O ★ L ★ O ★ G ★ Y

1992   • Sammy is traded to the Chicago Cubs for George Bell.

1993   • Sammy joins the 30-30 club with 33 home runs and 36 stolen bases.

1995   • Sammy is named to the National League All-Star Team for the first time.

1998   • Sammy slugs 66 home runs and wins the N.L. MVP award.

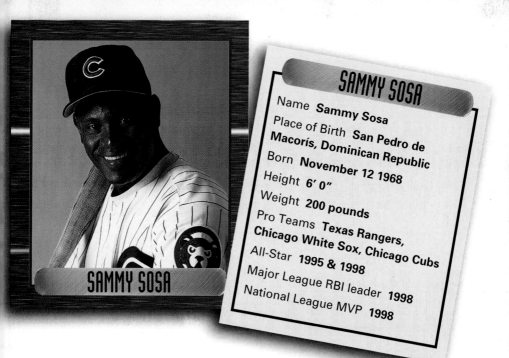

Name Sammy Sosa

Place of Birth San Pedro de Macorís, Dominican Republic

Born November 12 1968

Height 6' 0"

Weight 200 pounds

Pro Teams Texas Rangers, Chicago White Sox, Chicago Cubs

All-Star 1995 & 1998

Major League RBI leader 1998

National League MVP 1998

SAMMY SOSA

SAMMY SOSA

⭐ MAJOR LEAGUE STATISTICS ⭐

Season	Team	H	R	HR	RBI	SB	AVG
1989	Rangers/W. Sox	7	27	4	13	7	.257
1990	White Sox	124	72	15	70	32	.233
1991	White Sox	64	39	10	33	13	.203
1992	Cubs	68	41	8	25	1	.260
1993	Cubs	156	92	33	93	36	.261
1994	Cubs	128	59	25	70	22	.300
1995	Cubs	151	89	36	119	34	.268
1996	Cubs	136	84	40	100	18	.273
1997	Cubs	161	90	36	119	22	.251
1998	Cubs	198	134*	66	158*	18	.308
Total		1233	727	273	800	217	.264

* Led Major Leagues

ABOUT THE AUTHOR

Caleb MacLean is a sports researcher and writer who has worked on numerous books for children, including several titles in the Grolier All-Pro Biography series. He also has contributed to projects for Children's Television Workshop, ESPN, and The Walt Disney Company. A lifelong Cubs fan, Caleb now resides in Studio City, California. He has written two books in the Sports Stars series.